ULTIMATE THRILL SPORTS

SKYDIVING

By Lesley Gale

Gareth Stevens
Publishing

Please visit our web site at www.garethstevens.com
For a free catalog describing our list of high-quality books, call 1-800-542-2595 (USA) or
1-800-387-3178 (Canada). Our fax: 1-877-542-2596

Library of Congress Cataloging-in-Publication Date available upon request from publisher.

ISBN-10: 0-8368-8962-2   ISBN-13: 978-0-8368-8962-8 (lib. binding)

This U.S. edition copyright © 2008 by Gareth Stevens, Inc. Original edition copyright © 2007 by ticktock
Media Ltd., First published in Great Britain in 2007 by ticktock Media Ltd., Unit 2, Orchard Business
Centre, North Farm Road, Tunbridge Wells, Kent, TN2 3XF

ticktock project editor: Julia Adams
ticktock project designer: Sara Greasley
ticktock picture researcher: Lizzie Knowles
editor: Ben Hubbard

Gareth Stevens Senior Managing Editor: Lisa M. Guidone
Gareth Stevens Creative Director: Lisa Donovan
Gareth Stevens Graphic Designer: Giovanni Cipolla
Gareth Stevens Associate Editor: Amanda Hudson

Picture credits (t=top; b=bottom; c=center; l=left; r=right): Cover: Joel Kiesel/Getty Images. Erik Aasbarg:
45b. Airbourne Systems: 13t. Airtec: 21t. Alti-2: 21c. Felix Baumgartner: 54. Hans Berggren: 21b, 37b.
Bettmann/Corbis: 11cl. Fiona Birnie: 41t. Darren Birkin: 35b. Willy Boeykens: 6b, 14/15, 18t, 33t, 34/35t,
36, 41b. Bone Head: 18b. JC Colclasure: 27t. Rob Colpus: 60b. Corbis: 10t. Tony Danbury: 47t. Jay
Epstein: 55b. F.A.I: 60b. Andy Ford: 25c, 49t. Oliver Furrer: 53tr. Sarah Hall: 38b, 39bl, 39br. Mark Harris:
32t, 57t. Tony Hathaway: 42/43. Richard Hayden: 29bl. Ian (Milko) Hodgkinson: 59t. Ash Hollick: 47b.
Simon Hughes: 46. Jump Shop: 19t. Jupiter Images/Thomas Ulrich: 55t. Photograph by Norman Kent:
7b, 22/23, 29br, 56. Keith MacBeth: 28/29t. Peter Male: 48. Anton Malevsky: 28b. Michael McGowan:
30/31. Neil McLaren: 13b. Mike Mumford: 11tr. Francisco Neri: 16/17t, 26t, 27cl, 40t. Craig O'Brian: 37t,
52t. Dean O'Flaherty: 4/5, 6/7t, 44/45t. Johnny Panakis: 58. ParaSki.co.uk: 24t. Patrick Passe: 53cl.
Jason Peters: 40b. Photolibrary: 1, 33c. Grant Richards: 61b. Shutterstock: 2, 3, 20. Sky High
Entertainment Movies: 59b. Barbara Sokol/Beck Isle Museum/Sydney Smith: 9b. Square One: 19cr.
James Stevenson: 38/39t. Jack Sullivan/Alamy: 17b. ticktock Media Archive: 25t. Total Control: 19bl.
Martijn Van Dam: 50/51. Gary Wainwright: 16b, 34b, 44b. Simon Ward sward@airkix.com: 49b, 57b.
Wikipedia: 8t, 9t.

Every effort has been made to trace the copyright holders for the photos used in this book, and the
publisher apologizes in advance for any unintentional omissions. We would be pleased to insert the
appropriate acknowledgements in any subsequent edition of this publication.

Printed in the United States of America

1 2 3 4 5 6 7 8 9 10 09 08 07

Contents

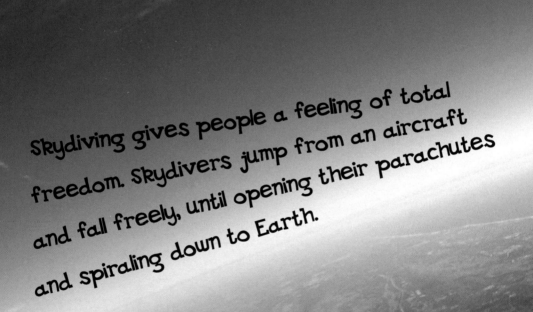

chapter 1: introduction

Skydiving gives people a feeling of total freedom. Skydivers jump from an aircraft and fall freely, until opening their parachutes and spiraling down to Earth.

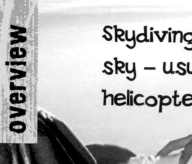
Skydiving is literally diving into the sky — usually from an aircraft, a helicopter, or a balloon.

Skydiving

Skydiving includes two types of activities: free falling and parachuting. First, divers fall freely through the air. They can do tricks on their own or hold onto others, building a formation that looks like a spider web in the sky. It is a great feeling to link up with friends and smile at one another a mile above the ground!

Parachuting

After the free fall, it is time to open the parachute. A parachute is also called a canopy. This part of the jump is called parachuting. The diver can choose to make a gentle landing, or he or she can swoop, traveling along the ground at high speeds before landing.

A free fall over Titusville, Florida

Skydiving is not for the faint of heart!

Mental Aspects

The decision to jump out of an aircraft should not be taken lightly. Skydiving can be dangerous, and there are risks involved. Of course, that risk is also what draws most people to the sport.

7

Leonardo da Vinci's parachute sketch (1483)

The story of parachuting began in the late 15th century, when the Italian inventor and artist Leonardo da Vinci sketched a parachute in his notebook.

Da Vinci's parachute was made of cloth stretched over a pyramid-shaped frame. His idea was to help people escape from burning buildings. A note read, "If a man is provided with a length of gummed linen cloth with a length of 12 yards on each side and 12 yards high, he can jump from any great height whatsoever without injury."

Sebastian Lenormand parachutes from
the Montpelier Observatory in 1783.

In 18th century France, Joseph Montgolfier tested different kinds of parachutes by dropping animals from rooftops. His colleague Sebastian Lenormand parachuted from the Montpelier Observatory in Paris and first used the word parachute. In French, parachute means "to shield a fall."

French balloonist Jean-Pierre Blanchard tried his parachute out on his dog before becoming famous doing his own exhibition jumps in England and France. Another pioneer from France, Andre-Jacques Garnerin, leaped from hot air balloons as high as 8,000 feet (2,438 meters) with a silk parachute. He developed a hole at the top to let air out and to stop it from oscillating (swinging like a pendulum). His wife, Genevieve Labrosse, and niece, Elisa, became the first women to parachute.

An early parachute jump from
a hot air balloon

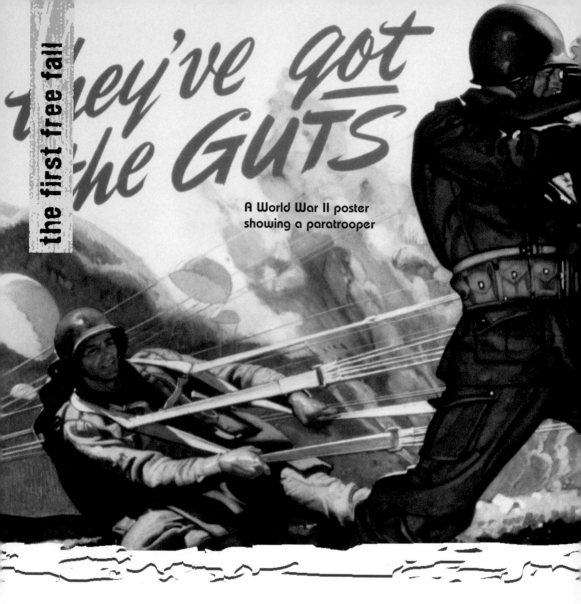

they've got the GUTS

A World War II poster showing a paratrooper

Georgia Broadwick was nicknamed "Tiny" because she was only four feet tall. Tiny started parachuting in 1907, at age 14, as part of a carnival act. She went up attached to a balloon, released her parachute, and floated down.

In 1914, Tiny demonstrated parachuting to the United States military. On one jump, the static line (a cord attached to an object, such as a plane, which opens the parachute automatically) became tangled. To free herself, she cut the line and pulled it manually, becoming the first person to free fall.

Leo Valentin jumps in his canvas wings for the first time in Villa Coublay, France (1950).

Georgia "Tiny" Broadwick

In 1950s, pioneering French "Birdman" Leo Valentin discovered many of the free-fall techniques that are still used in skydiving today. He found that the "stable" position (arms spread, belly down) could help prevent the diver from tumbling through the air. Valentin, a former paratrooper during World War II, was killed during a jump in 1956. It was a fate common to early skydivers. From 1930 to the early 1960s, many "birdmen" were killed in pursuit of new flying techniques.

The invention of the airplane brought new life to parachute development. Aircraft pilots needed a way to escape in case of an accident. Kaethe Paulus, a German woman, designed a parachute for the German Air Force. In World War I every German pilot was given one.

The para-commander
was a type of parachute
invented by
Pierre M. Lemoigne.

Para-Commander

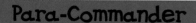

In the 1950s, silk parachutes were modified with holes to create
forward speed. This led to a generation of sport parachutes with a
bizarre pattern of slots, known as high performance rounds. The
para-commander shown above is an example. This type of parachute
was not used for very long because it often did not open properly.

Ram-Air

In the 1950s, a Florida man named Domina Jalbert adapted one of his kite designs to invent the ram-air, a rectangular parachute. In the 1970s the ram-air became the main parachute, and round parachutes were downgraded to reserves. Then the piggyback system was invented, which placed both main and reserve parachutes on the back, rather than the reserve on the front. In the 1980s the ram-air design became used for reserves.

A five-cell ram-air parachute

Ram-air Rectangular parachute rammed full of air

Sport

Ram-air parachutes originally had five sections, or cells. In the 1980s they became seven cells, which increased their speed. By the 1990s, they had become nine cells. This decade saw huge developments in all areas. Parachuting, invented for escape and safety, had become a state-of-the-art sport. It is so new that techniques, equipment, and training are still improving all the time.

A modern nine-cell ram-air parachute

chapter 2: all the gear

Parachutes are lightweight and very reliable. Today, two parachutes are smaller than one used to be! Skydivers wear many hi-tech gizmos to help keep them safe.

The modern ram-air parachute is inflated by air through the openings at the front, in the cells. These cells are closed at the back edge so the parachute becomes stable.

A ram-air parachute has a forward speed of about 30 mph (48 km/h), much faster than rounds, which travel at about 10 mph (16 km/h). It is the forward speed that keeps the canopy inflated. It is literally rammed with air. A ram-air canopy is made from nylon and coated with a special liquid to hold the air in. This keeps the parachute solid so it flies better. Skydivers choose a parachute size to suit their weight and ability.

The front view of a ram-air parachute

Venezuelan skydiving pro Francisco Neri with his ram-air parachute

Despite all this technology, skydivers always use a reserve parachute for backup. The main parachute and the reserve are packed in one neat container, one above the other. The systems are very reliable. Injuries or deaths are almost always due to personal error, not equipment failure.

Parachutes are being packed, with the main parachute in a black bag above the reserve.

Skydivers wear jumpsuits over their clothes so there is no loose material flapping over emergency handles. Jumpsuits are strongly made to withstand free fall speeds. They also help groups of people move at the same speed. Light divers wear tight, nylon jumpsuits so they fall faster. Heavier divers wear loose, cotton jumpsuits, giving them lots of drag.

Helmet

Helmets protect the head in case of collisions or hard landings. Some helmets include a video camera that records a jump from the diver's point of view.

Goggles

Some jumpers prefer a helmet with a visor. Others prefer an open-faced helmet and goggles. Both options protect the eyes from the wind. They keep the eyes from drying out and make it easier to see clearly.

Gloves

Thin leather gloves keep hands warm, protect from line burns, and give good grip for holding onto the aircraft.

Weights

Lighter jumpers may wear lead weights so they fall faster. The extra weight helps them fall at the same speed as heavier people.

Knife

Skydivers often wear a knife that has been designed to cut through tangled lines without damaging anything else.

After a free fall, the skydiver releases the main parachute. The parachute below is a seven-cell ram-air canopy with sub-divided cells.

Cells

Each cell of the canopy on this parachute is a different color. This makes the cells easy to identify.

Brake Lines

Brake lines connect the back edge of the canopy to the toggles.

Harness

The pilot is strapped into the harness. The harness is connected to the main and reserve parachutes.

Toggles

Toggles are the brakes of a parachute. The pilot pulls them to slow down, and pulling either one will steer the canopy.

Most skydivers wear an automatic activation device (AAD). This device operates the reserve if they fail to open the main parachute. The diver might have been knocked out, or not fully aware of the height he or she has reached. An AAD fires at around 750 feet (229 meters) if its user is still in free fall.

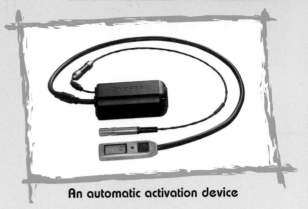

An automatic activation device

An altimeter

An altimeter shows the height above the ground. It is worn on the wrist or the chest strap. Some are audible altimeters, which are worn next to the ear. They give loud warning beeps. Others also record information, such as jumping altitude, free fall speed, and the height at which the parachute was opened. This data can be downloaded to a computer.

Inexperienced jumpers wear radios so an instructor can talk them through their parachute ride. Radios have also been used to coordinate groups of skydivers on world record attempts. Some divers have recently started using head-up displays, like the kind worn by jet fighter pilots. The altitude and free fall speed are projected into the view of the skydiver.

U.S. skydiver Craig Girard wears a head-up altitude display.

Skilled skydivers can accomplish amazing feats. The world's top pilots can fly in formation, do a 360° turn, and skim across the surface of a lake!

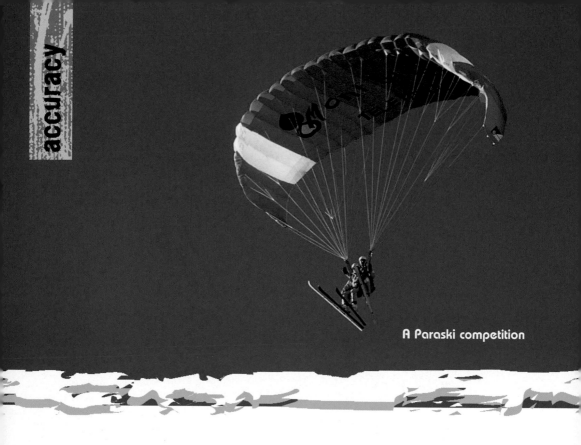

A Paraski competition

One type of canopy flight competition is accuracy. In accuracy competitions, each jumper tries to land as close to a target as possible. The target is a tiny disc just over an inch across, about the size of a man's thumbnail.

If you land on the target in a competition, you score a zero. If you land further away, the distance is your score. Accuracy competitions usually take place over two or three days, depending on the weather and the number of competitors. The standard is very high. At world level, there is often a jump-off to determine the champion. The world record for the most consecutive landings on a 1.18 inch (30 millimeter) disc in competition is 21, set by Russian Liubov Ekshikeeva, in 2005.

Cheryl Stearns

Cheryl Stearns is the most successful competitive skydiver in the world. She has been the U.S. women's accuracy champion a record 22 times. Her scores often beat the men as well as the women. Cheryl holds 30 world parachuting records and more than 70 gold medals for world and U.S. national championships. She has done more than 17,000 skydives – more than any other woman. Cheryl holds the female world record for doing the most skydives in 24 hours – 352!

Liz Danby shows off her vertical accuracy.

In Paraski competitions, skydivers jump onto the side of a ski slope and are scored for their accuracy. Then they slalom down a ski run and are scored on their times. The combined scores give the winner.

Extreme canopy piloting by
Canadian Jay Moledzki

Canopy piloting competitions have three areas: speed, distance, and zone
accuracy. In speed, the canopy pilots are scored on how fast they go.
After the skydive, they open their canopy and fly in a series of spirals to
build up speed. Then they fly parallel to the ground at a height of about
20 feet (6 m). This is called swooping. Pilots must pass through a start gate
set up at this height.

In distance, pilots fly parallel with the ground for as long as possible. The world
record is 495 feet (151 m), set by Canadian Jay Moledzki.

In zone accuracy, pilots go through a start gate and then try to land on a
target.

Jonathan Tagle

American Jonathan Tagle started skydiving late — at age 31 — but did 800 jumps in his first year. Now he has completed 5,000 jumps and is part of the best swooping team in the world. He was overall world champion in canopy piloting in 2005, also winning the speed and distance events. He became King of Swoop, U.S. National Champion, Pro Swoop Tour Champion, and European Swoop Champion. He also set two world records.

Freestyle canopy piloting by American Ian Bobo

Freestyle is a creative area of canopy piloting. The pilot is free to create a new move, a funny transition, or an artistic flourish. Judges score the landing for its difficulty, appearance, and originality.

It is easy to link canopies together. You can join them on top of each other, as a stack. You can link them side by side. If you combine the two methods, you can build all sorts of amazing formations.

In formation competitions, skydivers are judged on their ability to make a series of group formations in a set amount of time. Judges make their decisions based on video footage of the jumps.

In rotation competitions, the top person in the stack collapses his or her canopy, falls past everyone else, and joins the stack at the bottom. This is one rotation.

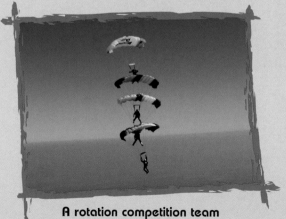

A rotation competition team

World record
formation over
Lake Wales, Florida

The best way to build a large formation is in a diamond. This is the most stable shape. The world record for a formation was set in 2005, with 85 canopies. The formation was 300 feet (91 m) high, 200 feet (61 m) wide, and weighed eight tons.

A close-up of a canopy formation

A world record formation attempt

chapter 4: free fall

Free fall is a unique experience, and does not feel like falling. The sensation is more like flying.

A skydiver free falls in stable belly-to-earth position

If you go into free fall curled up in a ball, you will tumble. But if you make your body streamlined, you can almost fly, without spinning or rolling over. This is called the stable position.

The most common dive position is the stable position, or belly-to-earth. The arched belly gives the air a smooth surface to flow over, like a badminton birdie. Skydivers in this position generally jump at 13,000 feet (3,963 m) and free fall for a minute, before opening their parachutes at 2,500 feet (762 m). Skydivers fall at a speed of about two miles a minute!

SKYDIVING

In a free fall dive, you can reach 200 mph (322 km/h).

The Stable Position

The inventor of the stable position, Leo Valentin, describes his first jump using it:

"I take up my position. Suddenly I have a sensation of great well-being. Had it not been for the wind I might be motionless in the sky, reclining face downward on the cushions of air through which I am plunging almost without stirring. It is so different from the normal twisting that for a moment I am scared. It seems impossible that it can be so easy, so agreeable, so intoxicating in its smoothness."

A birdie falling downward; the arrows indicate the air flow.

Once you can fall in the stable position, it is easy to change the angle of your body to move it through the air. You can then fly toward others and take hold of them to make formations.

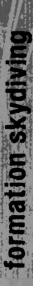

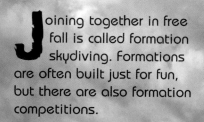

J oining together in free fall is called formation skydiving. Formations are often built just for fun, but there are also formation competitions.

Speed

The simplest formation competition is for speed. The winning team is the fastest to build a formation. Sequential competitions are more popular, where teams must build a sequence of different formations. A point is awarded for each formation built in a set time. A cameraperson flies with the team to record the action for the judges.

Teams

Teams contain four or eight people. They leave the aircraft linked together. Women have their own competition in the four-person event, but compete with the men if they wish. The eight-person event is mixed gender.

The British eight-way team launches a formation.

34

Skydivers in free fall
formation over
Lapalisse, France

Claire "Sparky" Scott

Claire "Sparky" Scott

British skydiver Claire Scott is the
only woman to have won five
world titles in four-way formation
skydiving. She has 4,000 jumps and
is an instructor. She has won two
Royal Aero Club awards and a host
of national and regional medals.
Sparky got her nickname by flying
into power lines, setting fire to a
field, and cutting off electricity to a
whole village!

With enough planning, it is possible to build very large formations. The world record, set in Thailand in 2006, is 400 skydivers!

Four hundred skydivers break the world record.

World Record

Five enormous Hercules aircraft taking 80 people each were used for the world record. The jump was from 23,000 feet (7,010 m). The air is very thin at this height, so the divers needed extra oxygen until they jumped. Men and women from 40 different countries participated in the dive.

The women's formation world record

Women's World Record

About one in five skydivers worldwide is female. Women have their own world record of 151 people, set in 2005 in California.

World Record Formations

Five Hercules planes load for
a world record attempt.

Year	Size	Location
1973	12	Arantchi Tachkent, Uzbekistan
1974	28	Ontario, California
1979	36	Muskogee, Oklahoma
1983	72	DeLand, Florida
1986	100	Muskogee, Oklahoma
1988	144	Quincy, Illinois
1992	200	Myrtle Beach, South Carolina
1999	282	Ubon Ratchathani, Thailand
2002	300	Eloy, Arizona
2004	357	Korat, Thailand
2006	400	Udon Thani, Thailand

Flying in free fall, in positions other than belly-to-earth, is called freeflying. In freestyle competitions, aerial gymnastics are carried out in free fall by the performer. The performance is recorded on film by a team member and scored by judges.

As well as the basic belly-to-earth position, there are other shapes that are stable in free fall. The head-down position flies very nicely. The downward speed is rapid so there is less free fall – just 40 seconds – before it is time to go belly-to-earth and open the parachute.

The head-down position

Head-down Stable freeflying position where the jumper is upside down, with the head pointing downward

Yoko Okazaki
performs a
freestyle position.

Freefly competitions involve teams of three. One team member wears a camera, the other two perform together. Judges score the routine for its technical and artistic content.

Other ways of flying are the sit-fly position (like sitting in a chair) or the stand-up.
When you can fly in each basic position, you can move easily from one to another.

A totem: one freeflyer stands on another's shoulders.

The sit-fly position

World Record

The head-down world record is 69 people. The record was set in Chicago in 2007, from 18,000 feet (5,486 m). Interest in freeflying has been on the rise. The record tripled in three years.

Divers building a head-down formation

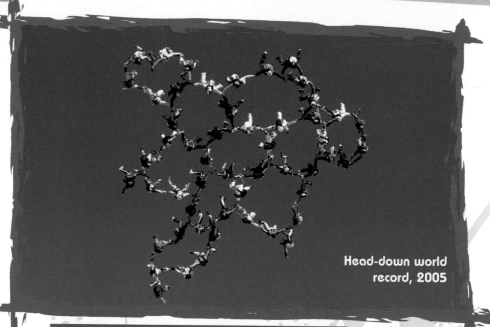

Head-down world record, 2005

Head-Down World Records

Year	Size	Location
2002	18	Perris Valley, California
2003	24	Sebastian, Florida
2004	42	Perris Valley, California
2005	53	Perris Valley, California
2007	69	Chicago, Illinois

Eli Thompson

Eli Thompson has co-organized and participated in every head-down world record. One of the inventors of freeflying, he started the Flyboyz team with two friends in 1996. The team became Freefly World Champions from 1997 to 2000. Eli hosts Discovery Channel's *Stunt Junkies* and works as a stunt skydiver. He has 14,000 jumps and has been U.S. National Freefly Champion, SSI Pro Tour Champion, ESPN World Champion, and has won the Space Games.

Eli Thompson

Yoko Okazaki and Axel Zohmann

Axis 21

Yoko Okazaki and Axel Zohmann are Axis 21 — a married freestyle team. Yoko performs beautiful flowing creations for the camera, worn on Axel's helmet in free fall. They are three-time world champions, hold two world records, and have won 11 international medals. Yoko is a former gymnast who has made more than 6,400 jumps.

Freestyle One person performs acrobatic maneuvers in free fall and another person films it.

41

chapter 5: getting started

It can definitely be scary to try something as extreme as skydiving, but there are safe ways to start. Here is someone on her second jump, with instructors "on guard" on either side. This is called accelerated free fall (AFF), one of three ways to try parachuting.

The three ways to start skydiving are: tandem, AFF, and static line. A tandem jump is in a dual harness with an instructor. An AFF jump is with an instructor on either side in free fall. A static line jump is on your own.

A tandem parachute and harness is made for two. People trying skydiving for the first time jump with an instructor. Because the instructor takes care of the life-saving essentials, the pre-jump instruction only takes 15 minutes. Tandems leave the aircraft at around 12,000 feet (3,658 m) and free fall for 30 seconds. The instructor then releases a tiny parachute called a drogue. This slows the pair down to the free fall speed that just one person would have.

A tandem instructor (top) and beginner (bottom) in free fall

A tandem skydive over Florida

In a tandem jump, the instructor opens the canopy at about 5,000 feet (1,524 m). A tandem parachute is about twice the size of a normal canopy. The toggles are designed so both people can fly it. A tandem is ideal for people who just want to try skydiving once.

A tandem lands in Voss, Norway.

Accelerated free fall (AFF) is the fastest way to take up skydiving. "Accelerated" refers to the learning process, which is quickest by this method.

An AFF jump over Kent, England

AFF Jumps

The first AFF jump is from 12,000 feet (3,658 m) with two instructors, one on either side. In free fall, the instructors communicate to the new diver with hand signals. The beginner opens the parachute at 5,000 feet (1,524 m). The instructors hold on until the canopy is open. They will open it if the inexperienced jumper doesn't. The jumper wears a radio and is guided by an instructor to land safely.

An AFF skydiver opening the canopy

Training

An AFF course takes a day of training and is usually only offered to adults. The full course is eight to ten jumps, after which the student is signed off as a qualified skydiver. The first three jumps are with two instructors. After that, there will be just one.

An AFF jump over Wiltshire, England

Qualifying

The AFF jumps cover specific skills but are adapted to suit the individual. Each person can learn at his or her own pace. Every jump is reviewed and is often videotaped for review. It is a very personal and motivating way to learn to skydive. You can be a fully qualified skydiver in three days!

Adults can do a static line jump from around 3,500 feet (1,067 m). A static line is attached to the aircraft and opens the parachute automatically. This gives the fun of the canopy ride without free fall. Once the canopy is open, the novice is talked down over a radio. It takes a day of training to be ready.

A static line jumper exits the plane above Cambridgeshire, England.

The first free fall lasts for five seconds.

First Free Fall

People who enjoy their first jump and want to take up skydiving do another 5 to 10 static line jumps. If these go well, they are cleared for their first AFF jump – which generally lasts for five seconds. The times in free fall are gradually extended until they are jumping for a minute. Once they have learned the basic skills, they are responsible for their own actions.

Wind Tunnels

Vertical wind tunnels simulate free fall. Skydivers use them to practice flying perfect competition routines. They help people who want to learn to skydive. In most places you must be at least 18 years old to jump out of a plane, but tunnels are open to younger people. You can learn to fly your body. This makes it much easier to jump out of a plane when the time comes!

A tunnel-flying skydiver

chapter 6:
extreme skydiving

Even with something as extreme as skydiving, some people will try to make it even more intense. Next we will look at some bold skydiving carried out by athletes who like living on the edge.

Dutch pro skydiver Martijn Van Dam jumps from a high-rise building. Stunts like this are generally illegal and usually not attempted by even experienced professionals.

World Champion skysurfer
Tanya Garcia-O'Brien

Skysurfers ride aerial waves on a surfboard thousands of feet up in the air. Skysurfing is extremely difficult and requires balance, coordination, and strength.

Skysurfing competition teams are made up of a skysurfer and a camera flyer. Creative filming can enhance the surfer's skills and make moves look even more spectacular. Judges score the routine for creativity, originality, and difficulty. They also score the filming, taking the creative camera work into account.

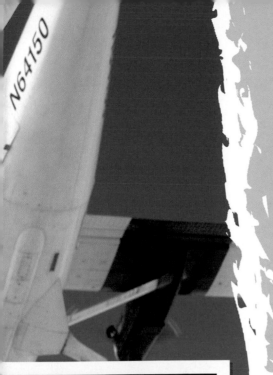

SKYDIVING

A skysurfer with a boogie board

Skysurfing Timeline

1980 – California skydivers first lie down on boogie boards in free fall.

1987 – Joel Cruciani from France stands up on a sky surfboard, using equipment from snowboarders.

1989 – In France, Patrick de Gayardon and Laurent Bouquet design an attach-and-release system for the feet.

1990 – Boards made of flexible rubber are jumped but prove too unstable to fly.

1991 – A light honeycomb aluminium and Kevlar structure makes boards more stable and better to fly.

1997 – First world championships in skysurfung take place in Finland.

A skysurfing trio

Sky surfboards look like skateboards with removable attachments for the feet. Skysurfing involves more risk than free fall. It is easy to lose control and end up in a spin. Skysurfers open their canopies higher to give them extra time to deal with problems. The board can be released in an emergency or for landing.

53

BASE jumping is skydiving from a fixed object. BASE is short for Building, Antenna (a mast), Span (a bridge), and Earth.

One Parachute

BASE jumping is more dangerous than standard skydiving. BASE jumpers rely on one parachute with no reserve. (There would not be enough time to open one.) They also risk colliding with the object they are jumping from. Their canopies may turn when they open, flying them straight into the object they are jumping from!

Austrian Felix Baumgartner prepares to BASE jump from the Christ the Redeemer statue in Rio de Janeiro, Brazil.

Climb to Jump

BASE jumpers find it thrilling to be closer to the ground. Climbing the object is part of the adventure and gives a good workout before the adrenaline rush of the jump. The sport is often practiced in beautiful settings such as the mountains in Switzerland or the fjords of Norway.

BASE jumping off the Eiger Mushroom in Switzerland

Underground Skydiving

A BASE jump at the Pit of the Swallows cave in Mexico

A cave in Mexico allows skydivers to jump underground! It has an opening at ground level and is 1,200 feet (366 m) deep. The cave is called Sótano de las Golondrinas, or Pit of the Swallows, because 80,000 birds live in the cave. More than 130 people have BASE jumped here. It is not for the timid. Divers must fly in a constant spiral to avoid hitting the walls!

For centuries, people have created elaborate winged contraptions. Many of the early pioneers, called "birdmen," died in their attempts to fly. They leapt from high places using aircraft and wings made from bones, feathers, wood, leather, canvas, and fabric.

A wingsuit skydive over the Florida Keys

Wingsuits

We have still not succeeded in building wings that allow us to fly like birds. But we now have wingsuits that double the free fall time. These suits have one huge wing from the wrists to the ankles. This grabs air like a sail in free fall. The result is a long flight at a slow downward speed. People who skydive with wingsuits are still called birdmen.

A flock over Cochstedt, Germany

Flocks

Birdmen and women fly in formations called flocks. They enjoy the extra time in free fall and the experience of whizzing around the clouds. BASE jumpers also love wingsuits. They reduce the risk as they double the free fall time and allow the jumper to fly away from the object.

Adrian Nicholas

Longest Free Fall

Wearing a wing suit, British skydiver Adrian Nicholas set a record for the longest free fall of four minutes, 55 seconds, in 1998. At the same time, Adrian made the longest human flight of 10 miles (16 kilometers) vertical distance. He was killed during a skydiving accident in 2005.

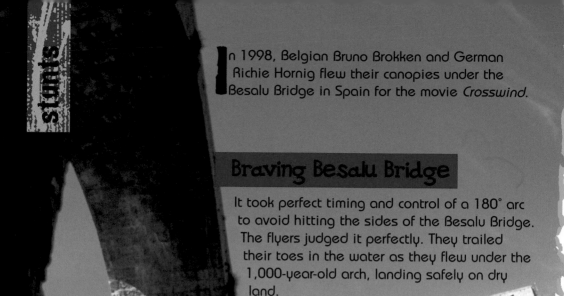

In 1998, Belgian Bruno Brokken and German Richie Hornig flew their canopies under the Besalu Bridge in Spain for the movie *Crosswind*.

Braving Besalu Bridge

It took perfect timing and control of a 180° arc to avoid hitting the sides of the Besalu Bridge. The flyers judged it perfectly. They trailed their toes in the water as they flew under the 1,000-year-old arch, landing safely on dry land.

Bruno Brokken swoops from Besalu Bridge in Spain.

Dave Morris lands on a hot air balloon.

Balloon Landing

In 2001, Dave Morris skydived from a helicopter at 10,000 feet (3,048 m), opened his canopy, and landed on top of a hot air balloon. Dave then jumped off the top of the balloon, going into free fall for the second time in one skydive! He opened a second parachute and landed safely on the ground in Nottinghamshire, England.

Adrian Nicholas and the da Vinci parachute

Da Vinci Parachute

In 2000, five hundred years after Leonardo da Vinci sketched the first parachute, his design was actually used. British skydiving pioneer Adrian Nicholas launched Leonardo's contraption from a hot air balloon over Mpumalanga, South Africa. It had been made using only tools and materials that would have been found in medieval Italy. Adrian commented, "I think da Vinci would have been pleased, even if the vindication of his idea came five centuries late."

1483 – The "father of the parachute," Leonardo da Vinci, sketches the first known parachute in the margin of his notebook.

1783 – French physicist Sebastian Lenormand jumps from the Montpelier Observatory in France, using a 14 foot (4.3 m) frame parachute.

1785 – Using a basket attached to a parachute, Jean-Pierre Blanchard drops his dog from a hot air balloon in France.

1797 – André-Jacques Garnerin, from France, makes the first jump using a parachute without a rigid frame. The homemade parachute is 8 feet (2.4 m) wide.

1808 – In the first recorded emergency jump, Jordaki Kuparento of Poland leaps from his burning hot air balloon over Warsaw. He is saved by his parachute.

1837 – Robert Cocking dies at a public show over Lea Green, England, in the first recorded parachuting death. His parachute falls apart during the event.

1890 – Paul Letterman and Kaethe Paulus, from Germany, invent a backpack-type container and start using parachutes folded into bags.

1895 – Kaethe Paulus demonstrates a "cutaway," releasing one parachute before opening a second. This solves the problem of tangling parachutes.

Growth of a Sport

The first world championships for parachuting took place in 1951, in Yugoslavia. It was attended by five nations. Gradually, more types of skydiving were invented and new competitions evolved.

Early world championships, 1981

1911 – The first airplane jump takes place over Venice Beach, California. Grant Morton jumps with a silk parachute in his arms, which he throws out as he leaves the plane.

1913 – In Los Angeles, Georgia "Tiny" Broadwick becomes the first woman to jump from an airplane.

1914 – Georgia "Tiny" Broadwick makes the first free fall jump. She cuts her static line free when it tangles around the airplane.

1947 – Leo Valentin invents the stable position.

1951 – Raymond Young first uses the term "skydiving," now an everyday term.

1960 – Colonel Joseph Kittinger makes the highest parachute jump. He steps out of a balloon gondola at 102,800 feet (31,333 m) over a New Mexico desert, making the longest free fall (at the time) of 4 minutes 36 seconds.

1998 – French trailblazer Patrick de Gayardon leaps from a Pilatus Porter aircraft above Lac de Bourget, flies alongside it wearing a wingsuit, and then gets back in.

1998 – British skydiver Adrian Nicholas makes the longest free fall. He falls for four minutes 55 seconds, using a wingsuit from 30,000 feet (9,144 m). He also makes the longest human flight, traveling 10 miles (16 km) horizontally.

Modern Skydiving

In 2006, the World Parachuting Championships included eight different events, with 25 competing nations. Areas covered freeflying, freestyle, skysurfing, canopy formation, and canopy piloting. This last competition was held in Vienna, Austria, over the Danube Tower, and watched by 15,000 spectators.

Canopy piloting at the 2006 World Parachuting Championships, in Vienna

Glossary

Accelerated free fall/AFF Individual course that teaches skydiving in 8 to 10 jumps

BASE jumping Jumping from a fixed object, instead of an aircraft of balloon. BASE is an acronym, a word made from the initial letters of the objects you could jump from: Building, Antenna, Span (i.e. bridge), Earth.

Birdman/woman A person who skydives in a wingsuit or, as a historical term, anyone who made wings and tried to fly

Canopy A parachute

Cells Sections of a ram-air canopy. They are open at the front to let air in and keep the canopy's shape and stability. The cells are generally subdivided into two or three sections.

Cut away Getting rid of the main canopy, usually when it has not opened properly, or is tangled around something

Drogue A small parachute used to slow down a falling object, such as a tandem pair in free fall

Emergency handles Located on the parachute harness for use if things go wrong. The cutaway handle gets rid of the main parachute, and the reserve handle opens the reserve parachute.

Extreme canopy flying Flying a parachute to gain maximum performance, usually making a complete spiral or two with the canopy to build up speed

Formation Two or more jumpers linked in free fall (formation skydiving) or under canopy (canopy formation)

Free falling Freely falling toward Earth

Freefly Free falling any way other than belly-to-earth

Head-down Stable freeflying position where the jumper is flying upside down in free fall, with their head pointing downward

Lines Pieces of thin cord which attach the parachute to the harness

Paratroopers Soldiers trained in parachuting. Paratroopers were first used extensively in World War II by Germany.

Pilot The person controlling the parachute (or aircraft)

Ram-air An aerofoil parachute, open at the front and closed at the back so that it is literally rammed full of air. Its shape is rectangular but slightly curved.

Reserve A second parachute worn in case the first (main) parachute does not open properly

Sequential A type of skydiving competition where there is a sequence, or series, of different formations to build, one after the other

Sky2surfing Skydiving while standing on a surfboard

Speed A type of skydiving competition where the aim is to be the fastest team

SSI Short for Skysurfing International, an international competition in skysurfing and freeflying that takes place in various locations all over the world

Stack A formation where ram-air canopies are linked vertically above each other. The top jumper's feet are hooked in the bottom person's lines

Static line A line attached to the aircraft, which pulls the main parachute out and open as the jumper leaves the plane

Swoop High speed landing generally performed under a high-performance canopy

Tandem A skydive with two people using a dual harness, with a very large parachute. It is generally an instructor taking a beginner on his or her first jump.

Wingsuit Suit with extra fabric "wings" that increase lift and free fall time, propelling its owner forward so he or she flies like a bird

Index

About the Author

Lesley Gale has been skydiving for more than twenty-three years and has made over 3,500 jumps. She has participated in eleven world records and won more than a hundred skydiving medals. For the last twelve years, Lesley has worked as the editor of *Skydive* magazine.